The Way Out is...Through

God is with you in your wilderness experience

40 Days of Inspiration

The Way Out is...Through

God is with you in your wilderness experience

40 Days of Inspiration

by L.T. Willis

Editor
Ray Glandon

Senior Publisher
Steven Lawrence Hill Sr.

Awarded Publishing House
ASA Publishing Company
Established Since 2005

A Publisher Trademark Cover page

ASA Publishing Company
Awarded Best Publisher for Quality Books 2008, 2009
105 E. Front St., Suite 205, Monroe, Michigan 48161
www.asapublishingcompany.com

All Rights Reserved. No part of this publication may be reproduced, stored in a retrieval system or transmitted in any form or by any means electronic, mechanical, photocopying, recording, taping, web distribution, information storage, or otherwise, without the prior written permission of the publisher. Author/writer rights to "Freedom of Speech" protected by and with the "1st Amendment" of the Constitution of the United States of America. This is a work of religious educational learning purposes. With this title page, the reader is notified that this text is an educational tool, and the publisher does not assume, and expressly disclaims any obligation to obtain and/or include any other information other than that provided by the author. Any belief system, promotional motivations, including but not limited to the use of non-fiction characters and/or characteristics of this book, are within the boundaries of the author's own creativity and/or testimony in order to reflect the nature and concept of the book.

Any and all vending sales and distribution not permitted without full book cover and this title page.

Copyrights©2012 L.T. Willis, All Rights Reserved
Book: The Way Out is...Through "God is with you in your wilderness experience"
Date Published: 01.29.12
Edition: 1 *Trade Paperback*
Book ASAPCID: 2380590
ISBN: 978-1-886528-16-1
Library of Congress Cataloging-in-Publication Data

This book was published in the United States of America.
State of Michigan

A Publisher Trademark Title page

Table of Contents
THE WAY OUT IS...THROUGH – **40 Days of Inspiration**

Foreword .... (a)

Introduction .... (i)

Prayer before beginning devotional ....(vii)

Day 1   *No Letdowns* 1

Day 2   *Get Fit* 4

Day 3   *Take Cover* 7

Day 4   *Why are you really hurting?* 11

Day 5   *A Direct Witness* 14

Day 6   *On Purpose* 17

Day 7   *A Tree is worth a thousand words* 21

Day 8   *Seeing beyond what you see* 24

Day 9   *Recover what you've lost* 28

Day 10 *What goes up, must come down* 33

Day 11 *Light it Up* 36

Day 12 *Use Your Bounce* 39

Day 13 *Immunity* 42

Day 14 *When I see Jesus* 46

Day 15	*You are valuable*	49
Day 16	*Got Protection?*	53
Day 17	*Enough is Enough*	56
Day 18	*Reaching Your Potential*	59
Day 19	*L. I. G. it*	62
Day 20	*I'm Listening*	65
Day 21	*Flashback, don't look Back*	68
Day 22	*The Crossover*	71
Day 23	*What's your sign?*	74
Day 24	*Tracks in the snow*	77
Day 25	*Be careful*	80
Day 26	*Go to church*	83
Day 27	*Keep on praising*	86
Day 28	*Leave the light on*	89
Day 29	*Victory is mine*	91
Day 30	*I'm not worthy*	94
Day 31	*A job to do*	97
Day 32	*God did it*	100
Day 33	*Divine Intervention*	103
Day 34	*Take Control*	106
Day 35	*Activate your faith*	110
Day 36	*Get Up*	113
Day 37	*No Wrinkles*	116

Day 38	*Yes you can*	119
Day 39	*Comfort Zone?*	122
Day 40	*Through it All*	125
Conclusion		128
Prayer		132
Special Acknowledgements		133

The Way Out is...Through

God is with you in your wilderness experience

40 Days of Inspiration

by L.T. Willis

FOREWORD

When should parents take credit for what their children are doing? A parent should only want what's best for their children. Sometimes parents try and steer their children in a certain direction. God has required parents in Proverbs 22:6 to train up a child in the way that he should go, and when he gets old he will not depart from it. My wife Janice and I have strived at doing this with each of our children. They each have special gifts from God. I have seen God work tremendously with LaThomas in ministry and music. When he told the family that he was writing a book of inspiration, I was proud as a parent. I was also proud that he was listening to the voice of God, having no idea that it would be this complete and inspiring. When he asked me to read The Way Out is Through, I was touched. When he asked me to write the foreword, I was blown away. I have heard LaThomas preach many sermons. I have sat in on his teachings. But when I began reading this book,

I realized at that point that this book was written by LaThomas, but the Holy Spirit is the co-author. I've read many journals and devotionals, but very few have the power and blessing of this book. As I read through this book, I kept thinking about his first writings from elementary school, middle school, high school, college, and grad school. But this piece of work is different. The material in this book goes beyond schooling; it's more of wisdom. I kept thinking to myself, only God can give a 26 year old so much wisdom. LaThomas hasn't lived long enough to be writing in this manner!

After reading the introduction, I was equipped and ready for a 40 day journey. So many people stop in the middle and never finish the course. But before you stop, you need to know that the way out ... is through. Relationships, schools, finances, sickness, loneliness, whatever the struggle may be, reading the introduction alone will equip you for a 40 day wilderness experience. I was moved and blessed as I read through each day. Every day is supported with scripture references from the Bible and practical examples to serve as an easy read.

If you take time to read this book and pray as you read, the Holy Spirit will bless you on your 40-day journey. In any situation that you may find yourself in, I believe the Holy Spirit will comfort you by the words of LaThomas. It doesn't matter your social status or spiritual status, there is a word for you in "The Way Out is ... Through," as we all will experience the ups and downs that come with life. I'd recommend you sharing this book with your family and friends.

Rev. Arthur C. Willis, Sr.
Senior Pastor
Pentecost Missionary Baptist Church

(d)

INTRODUCTION

Come into His marvelous light! It's so good to be on the Lord's side! When praises go up, blessings come down! Jesus loves you! We all have heard this proclamation from scriptures and testimonies. And they are affirmative. Jesus is the light of the world, and He is marvelous. I'd rather accept the gift of eternal life than to be condemned to Hell. We often fail to acknowledge when facing doubt, defeat, and discouragement, that these seasons of life are what being a Christian is about. For some, it's so easy to give up on being like Christ. As a result, some bail out on commitments, relationships fall apart, devotion to God slacks, and faith decreases. Who in the world stops in the middle of the car wash because they don't like the way the car looks in the process? In fact, if you attempt to stop the car, you could cause damage to your vehicle because it would be off course. Being a Christian works the same way. Sometimes we need to be cleansed as David said in Psalms 51:10, "Create in me a clean heart and renew a right spirit within me." So we go through this spiritual car wash every now and then to get cleansed. In the process things may look crazy, cruel, and catastrophic, but if you bail out, you may cause damage to your purpose by brushing up against the wrong people, places, or paths.

The cost of discipleship must be counted. Christ had enemies because of who He said He was. We, too, will have the same enemies and distractions for our belief in Him, just because of who we say we are. Sometimes we will experience seasons where we feel as if we have been defeated. Sometimes God will test our faith by putting us in situations where only He can resurrect us. But we have to remember that we have the victory through Christ Jesus. Relying on the word of God will smooth the journey in the rocky, rigid, and rough season of our lives.

Let's think about physical exercise for a moment. We may suffer an injury because we aren't in shape to handle the task. Beloved, God will allow injury so that we become motivated to work our faith into shape. As a result, we're careful not to suffer the same injury in the future.

So, you're in your wilderness as the children of Israel were. Wilderness is synonymous with the word "wild." We refer to the word "wild" as a state of disorder. As children of the true and living God, we are subject to suffer anomie, abnormalities, and adversity. Like the children of Israel, some of us will become frustrated, fractured, and fragile. You may conclude that you are better off in the land of not enough (Egypt). The children of Israel didn't understand God's timing, just as many of us don't. I've had my share of experiences where I wanted to give up, throw in the towel, and bail on some commitments that I had made with God. But I kept hanging on as long as I could until I got my breakthrough. I realized that, although I was in a place of disappointment, God was still giving me just enough to make it through. So as I went through, I came out. He gave me the words in this devotional. The question many believers often ask is, "How do I get out of this?" We must answer this question by proclaiming that it's by the power of the God in me that I can make it through, and this is my way out! Shift your focus! Don't dwell on the numerous ways you can change the situation. Focus on how to get through your crisis or conflict at hand. There's purpose along the way and a message at the end of the tunnel. Don't get sidetracked and derailed; you may miss your moment of breakthrough and destiny. Stepping out of the will of God before the time is up isn't a breakthrough; it's a break-a-way! Don't break down before you break through. Your breakthrough is on the other side of the wilderness, but you must go through it to get to it.

PRAYER

Say this prayer before beginning this devotional:

Father, it's in the name of Jesus that I come before you. Father, I thank you for life. Father, you are the God of everything, even my problems. You are a great and mighty God. There is none like you. Father, I'm engaged in a battle, but You're bigger than the battle. Father, I'm in the midst of a storm. Be my umbrella of faith. Father God, give me strength when I'm weak. Straighten me out when I'm bent. Help me to make it thru without throwing in the towel. I understand that I don't make it through without moving. So God, give me the power to walk it out. Thank you, Father, for providing me with the greatest example of your power. You gave the world your Son, Jesus Christ, who knew no sin, but took on mine at the cross on Calvary's mountain. You showed me how you can resurrect any situation by Christ's crucifixion and resurrection from the dead. Father, that shows me that you can put light in any dark situation. Help me to see the light by guiding me out of my wilderness experience. When I don't feel like reading this devotional, remind me why I should. Thank you God. Amen.

DAY 1
No Letdowns!

He only lets you down when you allow pride to build you up!

-Trust in the Lord with all thine heart and lean not to your own understanding. And in all your ways acknowledge Him and He shall direct your paths.

- Proverb 3:5,6

To love God is to trust Him. Today, so many of us have put our trust into tangible things, which won't inherit the Kingdom of God. We trust the internet and cell phones, banks and hospitals. Women trust men, men trust women, and the two are imperfect beings. Therefore, don't trip when people let you down and break your trust. Don't expect them to be 100% trustworthy because they're not God. Where there are no expectations, there are no disappointments.

Many people become stressed out because someone who is imperfect let them down. When you don't expect something to happen, you haven't built up any anxiety for expectation; therefore, you are not disappointed in the result. This proverb teaches us to engage all of our heart in trusting God. We have to allow our trust for God to supersede the trust that we have for man. Just like you and I, people are imperfect. Being let down happens occasionally. Today, know that God will never let you down!

He leads us and guides us. Our job is to trust that He knows what He's doing. After all, He created the earth and everything in it, so He knows the path. All you have to do is acknowledge Him. Stay on course. You never know what God is keeping you from and setting you up for. Timing is everything.

As you trust the barricades and construction cones to guide you on road detours, use the same confidence, faith, and trust that God will guide you away from destruction in the midst of your construction. Don't put all your trust in yourself! When you think you have everything figured out, you're getting in the way of God and not in the will of God.

It's impossible to be the best person we can be without getting closer to Christ. He's the source of our strength!

-The Lord is my light and my salvation; whom shall I fear?
The Lord is the strength of my life; whom shall I be afraid?
-Psalms 27:1

God is able to illuminate your paths and deliver you from destruction, so who can stand against you? He'll show you where to go and keep you from getting lost. As followers of Christ, we benefit from establishing a relationship and keeping a connection with God. So many times people fail to count the cost of discipleship. Upon the first letdown, they give up on their faith. We all may know someone or may be that person who was on fire for God but allowed variables to put the fire out.

When things didn't go the way that they planned, believers pouted and polluted their minds with painful thoughts and paralyzing perceptions. God has not given us the Spirit of fear but of love, **power**, and a sound mind (2 Timothy 1:7) Being an athlete, I've learned that when we want to get physically stronger, we exercise physically! Many lift weights to get stronger while others ride bikes to increase stamina. If you want to get stronger mentally, you read more books and develop better study habits. To get stronger spiritually, you must exercise spiritually. Many people fail to continue dieting habits of work-out plans because they lose motivation.

Most of the time when there is an internal or external motivator, the individual is consistent in working out, thereby reaching the goals that were set prior to exercising. Exercise your faith by being motivated by the facts that God sent His Son, Jesus, to save the world from sin. You are victorious through Him (1 Corinthians 15:57). When you strengthen your faith in God, you become fearless, faithful, and focused in your life. Stick close to Him, and watch God maximize your potential!

DAY 3
Take Cover!

A house is under construction without a roof! It's incomplete without its covering! Are you covered? Are there any leaks in your roof! God is my covering!

-He who dwells in the secret place of the Most High shall abide under the shadow of the Almighty
-Psalms 91:1

When storms move into our area of residence, meteorologists alert us of a warning or watch and to take cover. In fact, schools are required to provide drills on taking cover in case a tornado or severe storm passes. In other words, they practice preparation, just in case. When winds blow the roof off of our homes or buildings, we label the event a disaster. A missing roof causes the inside of the building's structure to be exposed to the external environment, allowing anything that's not supposed to be there to come inside. Even when there are small leaks in the roof, we find buckets to prevent water from the outside from damaging what's on the inside. We must use the same precaution with our spirituality. When we're not covered, our lives are exposed to the external environment the world has to offer. This is one way the enemy has been able to influence are youth in this generation. Figuratively speaking, momma made daughter go to church 5 days a week when daughter was a child. But when daughter grew up, daughter strayed away from the church house. And now that daughter has had a child, she dismisses the traditional Church childrearing and provides her child with choices on whether or not he or she wants to go to church. As a result, the child's covering isn't a priority.

Many of the world's youth would rather blend in and conform to what's outside the house. However, greater is He that is in you, than he that is in the world (1 John 4:4). We know that the devil is the prince of darkness (this world), but God is greater than the world, He has overcome the world. The problem is … when we don't have God in us, we are exposed to the enemy. When we're not covered by the shadows of the Almighty God and not dwelling in His secret place, we expose ourselves to the enemy, thereby allowing him to use us as one of his imps to carry out his demonic mission. Fix the leaks in your life.

DAY 4
Why are you really hurting?

Pain is a symptom of the issue!

-To the woman He said, I will greatly multiply your sorrow and your conception; In pain you should bring forth children
-Genesis 3:16

Pain isn't the initial problem, but it's the effect of a cause. Consider your causes. Beloved, causes can come in a variety. The cause of your pain could be _____ (you fill in the blank). Or the cause can be doubt, peer relations, family, spouses, significant others, drugs, alcohol, fornication, just to name a few. Each cause in this list can ultimately be detrimental to your purpose in life. Now is not the time to test your pain threshold. Don't get comfortable in pain.

Most people who survive pain believe there's a healing coming, and that belief carries them through the process. The woman in Genesis 3:16 is Eve, who has committed the sin of eating the forbidden fruit that God told her and Adam not to indulge in. As a result, man will forever work by the sweat of his brow and woman bear pain in childbirth. The pain is the result of the disobedience, which is the real problem. We sometimes experience hurt but allow ourselves to be overcome with the pain of the hurt and fail to acknowledge the cause. If we can get to the root reason of the issue, then we can begin to apply coping strategies. Be encouraged when you're paining, because, as the word of God implies, the woman will bring forth children in pain, which means she'll be fruitful when the pain is over. God uses pain so that we can depend on Him and He can reveal His healing power! No pain, no gain!

Day 5
A Direct Witness

Scars are evidence of your healing, so be encouraged. When rough times arise, look at your scars and recollect how God healed each one!

-For He bruises, but He binds up; He wounds, but His hands make whole.   -Job 5:18

When I was a little boy, I fell off my bike. I have that very painful memory that surfaces each time I look at that scar which is covered by my goatee. No matter what I do to my face, the scar remains there. It reminds me of my mistake of riding too fast on the sidewalk. Reckless riding!

When it comes to a wound, the healing process includes some pain. But the pain means the wound is getting better. However, don't leave the wound untreated, lest it will be infected. Cover the wound with ointment and a bandage. God will provide an anointing for you and cover you and heal you, while leaving the scar as evidence that you've been healed. Life will bring about painful experiences, but remember how God got you through them. Don't focus on how you got the scar. That can lead to depression, doubt, or dismay. So what if it's your fault that you have the scar! Forget about that part! Remember the best part about a scar! It always heals if we leave it alone and let

God handle it! Therefore, when faced with new obstacles and challenges you can have confidence in knowing that God will see you through and bring you out. Have faith knowing that each wound may take a different time to heal, but it will heal. This variety in healing time will equip you with a tolerance for pain. The trying of your faith worketh patience.

Day 6
On Purpose

Destination is from the root word Destiny. Once you decipher your Destiny, get in route to reach your final destination and recognize purpose!

-Trust in the LORD with all your heart, And lean not on your own understanding; In all your ways acknowledge Him, And He shall direct your paths.

-Proverbs 3:5-6

As a child traveling to Georgia with my parents, we rode down the interstate through several Southern states. It was then when I noticed the

Appalachian Mountains cutting across the interstate. I wondered what dad was going to do as I examined the map that showed the interstate cutting through these states without roadblocks. I noticed that the mountains were too big and too round for us to go over or under. We had to go through to continue our trip.

Many people become confused with the meaning of the words purpose and destiny. I've considered that purpose is the road traveled to destiny. We, as children of God, have to realize that everything happens for a reason. Paul wrote in Romans 8:28, "And we know that all things work together for the good to those who love God, to those who are called according to His purpose." Everything that happens to you on your way to reaching your destiny is purposeful to you reaching your destiny, so do not give up. So many times we become easily frustrated with life and get off course. While driving to a desired destination, no matter the number of potholes, narrowed lanes, or accidents there are, we recognize it as something that has happened that we can't do anything about except press on toward the destination. We trust in God and not ourselves, that we may be able to follow His leadership to our desired direction.

It is extremely important, however, that we acknowledge God and consult with Him. You would be extremely lost trying to get to a foreign place with no road map. God has designed a road map for our lives. Get in His will, recognize the things to come are on purpose, and you will reach your destiny. Today, know that doing the *right* thing is the only way you can reach destiny. Consider direction. Time does not move unless it ticks toward the *right*. You don't arrive anywhere in the United States of America and other parts of the world without traveling on the *right* side of the road. If you're right with God, everything that happens to you happens on purpose so that you reach your destination.

Day 7
A Tree is worth a thousand words

I love trees! Beloved, God will strip you of some things to prepare you for your season of new growth!

-To everything there is a season, A time for every purpose under heaven.   -Ecclesiastics 3:1

You have to proclaim just as you may when you're feeling on top of the world, that it's your season. Usually this cliché is appropriate when everything is going according to plan in regards to our wants and needs. The money isn't funny, the change isn't strange. We wake up smiling. We lie down smiling. Everything is copasetic. Some even feel larger than life itself. We seldom embrace the opposite, however. It is equally important to understand and make it known it's your season when you're experiencing tough times and difficulties. Things are going to happen in life that we have no control over. We may even see some things coming our way, and there's nothing we can do to prevent it. All we can do is control our character in our crisis.

Consider the tree. A good tree generally stands in inclement weather conditions. It bears all rain, sleet, hail, and snow. Sometimes insects and animals latch on to the tree and use it as environmental support. My brothers and sisters, please be like this tree. No matter what your situation may be, you can endure it as the tree does. You must continue to stand like that tree planted by the rivers of the waters. So if you're catching hell right now, change your perception and mentality. Look at is as God preparing you to receive what He has next in His perfect plan for your life.

DAY 8
Seeing beyond what you see

In Isaiah 6, he states that it was in the year King Uzziah died that he saw the Lord. Sometimes in life it takes us losing something to see God!

In the year that King Uzziah died, I saw the Lord sitting on a throne, high and lifted up, and the train of His robe filled the temple.

-Isaiah 6:1

Don't focus on what's gone. Focus on what's coming! Your sight is a sense that enables neurons to travel to the brain to communicate a message of what it is that you are seeing. Imagine standing in the middle of a two-way street as a vehicle is passing by. Sight has us to focus on the back of a car departing from where we are standing, but also sight enables us to recognize another vehicle coming toward us which is seen further away from the vehicle that has left us.

Many times, we become overwhelmed about the fact that we've lost something or someone. Because of the attachments that we have maintained with someone or something, it may seem impossible to exist without them.

However, as children of God, we do know that all things work together for the good to those who love God and to those who are called according to His purpose (Romans 8:28).

Remember, things happen because they are supposed to happen. We can often become fixated on individuals or situations to where we miss God all together. Other people begin to become our center of attraction.

Remember, God has a jealous attribute to His character (Thou shall have no other god before me). In life, we may not be reaching our full potential or purpose that God has designed for us, and it takes Him removing that influence or focal point in order for us to get where we need to be. On this journey, remember that some things or people may be taken away, but be not dismayed. That removal will provide you with the opportunity to be cleansed. Devote your service to the true and living God and eventually proclaim, like Isaiah, "Send me Lord, I'll go."

When you lose something valuable, you search for it. So many saints have lost their religion and have failed to recapture it. Diligently seek God!!! Get your rewards by seeing beyond what's before you!

When you lose something valuable, you search for it. So many saints have lost their religion and have failed to recapture it. Diligently seek God!! Get your rewards!

Either what woman having ten pieces of silver, if she lose one piece, doth not light a candle, and sweep the house, and seek diligently till she find it? And when she hath found it, she calleth her friends and her neighbours together, saying, Rejoice with me; for I have found the piece which I had lost.

- Luke 15:8-9

It's natural that when you lose something valuable, you search for it. Whether its money, cars, clothes, jewelry, people, wallets, wedding rings, keys, or other items, we're swift to find that thing with a sense of urgency. On the contrary, when some lose their purpose in life, they fail to recover it. Too often, some Christians have allowed themselves to become occupied with pleasurable people or things, that they've been derailed on their spiritual journey and have lost faith in Christ. At times, the facts of life have caused many saints to have lost their religion and unfortunately, they have failed to recapture it.

I have found that when a person loses something, they will retrace their steps. At times, some are confident that they've placed that very thing in a specific area. However, the longer it takes to find the lost item, if you're not careful, anger and frustration will surface. Consider the woman in Luke 15:8. Jesus chose to use a woman who lost a coin in her own home. It's sad to say, but there are many church-goers who've lost purpose and some even faith in Christ, while attending church religiously. How does one get lost spiritually when they attend church regularly? Many are distracted, which is a tool of the enemy. Satan comes to kill, steal, and destroy, and he does it by distracting us from our purpose and gets us out of the will of God. If he can distract you, he can destroy you.

So how do you find the faith that you've lost? How do you recover that piece of you, that has left you empty? The bible says the woman lit a candle. A candle is lit as a source of light in dark places. Whatever is in darkness is overshadowed by darkness. Sometimes people lose value or have lost their faith because darkness has overshadowed their lives. When this is the case, you must launch an environmental cleansing effort.

Have you ever noticed that when we lose something at home, the house gets cleaned up? We're exposed to dirt that we have walked over daily. Beloved, on this spiritual journey, in recovering your purpose, value, and faith, you must cast a light on darkness or whatever isn't pure in your life, so that your value is recovered! There are some people who have lost their identity because they have been distracted by the enemy. This parable implies that that which was lost is valuable, and because it was lost it took the identity of the environment it was lost in. We take on the identity of what we are consumed by. But when the environment is cleansed the valuable is recovered.

DAY 10
What goes up, must come down!

Sowing & reaping is a very simple process. If you sow happiness or peace, that's what you will reap. The problem ... is people don't possess what they need to sow.

7) Do not be deceived, God is not mocked; for whatever a man sows, that he will also reap. 8) For he who sows to his flesh will of the flesh reap corruption, but he who sows to the Spirit will of the Spirit reap everlasting life.
-Galations 6:7-8

Depending on your experience, some of you may have heard this scripture used most often with finances. However, this is not the only place where the scripture applies. I'm a living witness that can say, where I've sown happiness, I have in some way reaped happiness. It may have gone unnoticed right away, but after a while, I was able to assess why a person acted kindly toward me.

Wouldn't your life, even your time in your spiritual wilderness, be much better if everyone sowed happiness and love into your life? I'm willing to say yes. However, the reality is, not everyone possesses what they need to sow. Aside from God's grace, before you can began to reap, according to the scripture, you have to sow! Let's think practically about this concept. If you decided to take off work for a whole week without using any vacation days, would you expect to get a paycheck for that week? Beloved, we have to put into practice the things which we wish to receive. If you want people to love you, love others. If you want people to bless you with gifts, try giving first. Jesus said it best in Luke 6:38, "Give, and it will be given to you: good measure, pressed down, shaken together, and running over will be put into your bosom. For with the same measure that you use, it will be measured back to you."

Motel 6 leaves the light on for you! Too many Christians have become motion censored!

-Ephesians 5:1-20

A light blends with lights and is always noticed in the midst of darkness. Is yours? Is your light on a time schedule, like every Wednesday night and Sunday morning or when there's a gospel event? Or, is your light ever shining? Is your light motion censored (only comes on when someone holy is in your presence)? Guess what? If you've been crucified with Christ, then there should be a light ever shining from you because we do know that the Son never stops shining. According to Paul's letter to Galatians, "it is not I but Christ that lives in me (2:20)." In Genesis 1:3-5, God saw the light, and He perceived it as good.

My brothers and sisters, you are valuable. God divided light and darkness. So while your friends, family, or co-workers are doing anything and everything, you are separated from that. Jesus said to let your light so shine before all men in Matt. 5:14, telling his disciples who they are and that they cannot be hidden because they were separated from the world from the beginning of time. Jesus said you are the light of the world, and a city on hill cannot be hidden. Now is not the time to hide! Your life, your family, and your friends are depending on you. People don't stare at lights in the rooms, they focus on what the lights illuminate and allows them to see. Your works will help people in your life see the goodness of Jesus Christ. It's the time to be bold and to stand out. During your time in your spiritual wilderness, don't try and blend in, be noticed!

DAY 12
Use Your Bounce

Rejection is sometimes a plan that God has in our lives to see how we're going to bounce back. It's a horrible feeling, but God has something better.

"11) He came to His own, and His own did not receive Him. 12) But as many as received Him, to them He gave the right to become children of God, to those who believe in His name:"

-John 1:-11-12

You might say in order for something to bounce, it had to be dropped. You're absolutely right! Let me tell you, I know what it feels like to be dropped. Have you ever been dropped when it seemed like you were doing everything right? Sometimes in life, what we think is the right move, is not necessarily God's move. Beloved, any move contrary to God's move, is the wrong move. Sometimes in life God leads us down the path of rejection to reveal His glory. Examine the reference scripture. God's plan was that salvation is a free gift for everyone to accept. Jesus was rejected by His own so that salvation would be granted to the Gentiles as well as the Jews. Thank God for the rejection.

Maybe you feel like you have been rejected by someone or something. It is important not to fall victim to depression and weaken your physical and mental strength. Instead, look at rejection as God positioning us to the right door of opportunity. I'm a living witness that God will set you back for a comeback just to remind us that He has our back. Sometimes we seek out what's behind door number 1 when God has designed a plan for us which is behind door number 2. Therefore, the rejection allows us to get back in His plan and on His timing. Rejection is also a timing issue. Sometimes we face rejection because it's not God's timing for us to knock at door number 1. Consider your rejection as an opportunity for someone else's breakthrough. In your spiritual wilderness don't be discouraged by rejection, be encouraged that you're back on track. What God has for you is indeed for you and only you!

Immunity is not accepting the illness; it's being able to handle it at its approach so that you are untouched.

"Do not touch My anointed ones, And do My prophets no harm."

-Psalms 105:15

In your wilderness you are going to encounter experiences with individuals who are demonically influenced to defeat and destroy you. There will be people in your life that are only interested in getting close to you to tear you apart. Please believe me that when you make up your mind that you are going to be sold out for Christ, a bullseye is on your back. Yes, your life is a target for the enemy.

As long as you're playing on the enemy's team, there's no reason to recruit you. But when you live right, Satan comes looking for you. Therefore, I'd like to suggest that some people are like the flu virus. They're in your life for a season to infest you with negativity, doubt, or any works of evil. Because God has chosen you and you have answered the call to discipleship, you're protected. The writer of this Psalm is speaking of the covenant that God made with Abraham, Isaac, and Jacob for their devotion to Him. God allows for us to go through certain things in our lives so that the next encounter won't affect us because of our spiritualized immune system.

Now, you may be saying to yourself, I've experienced things in the past that I'm finding it hard to become immune to. Consider the flu shot! When an individual receives a flu shot, this doesn't mean that they can waste away in bacteria or walk in differing climates not dressed accordingly. They don't socialize and encompass themselves with germs. The shot is designed so that in their casual presence of germs, they are not affected. What I'm saying is, though you may encounter negativity and sometimes it seems unavoidable, this doesn't mean you conform to negativity. This doesn't mean you embrace doubtful, deceiving, and destructive people in your space. It simply means you're untouchable!

Send a text message to your problem, and type "Can't touch this!"

Day 14
When I see Jesus!

Christians are windows through which Jesus shines. Can people look at you and see Jesus?

I have been crucified with Christ; it is no longer I who live, but Christ lives in me; and the life which I now live in the flesh I live by faith in the Son of God, who loved me and gave Himself for me.

-Galatians 2:20

The song writer says, "When I see Jesus, it will be AMEN." So why do Preachers and worship leaders have to beg for people to say AMEN in church? Perhaps some haven't seen Him in those whom He should be clearly seen; therefore they won't say AMEN. On your journey consider this: when a window is being cleaned, it is being sprayed with chemicals to cut through dirt to produce a better shine when wiped. The process of spraying windows isn't pleasant. Upon the first spray, it looks worse than when the process began. In order for someone to see Jesus in you, you have to go through a process of being cleansed. Certain things in your life are designed to cut through what's dirty, and anything that cuts can cause friction and perhaps pain. You may become frustrated and fractured when striving for Christ to be visible through you, but know that it's only in the process.

Beloved, in your spiritual wilderness, learn that you may be the closest opportunity someone has to meeting Jesus. You wouldn't want to be held accountable because you treated your Christianity as a wardrobe and only put in on display every other week.

Day 15
You are valuable!

Have you ever found loose change? A beat up busted penny that has made it down through the years is still valuable! No matter what you've been through, you're valuable.

"But you are a chosen generation, a royal priesthood, a holy nation, His own special people, that you may proclaim the praises of Him who called you out of darkness into His marvelous light"   *-1 Peter 2:9*

Pennies are cast into fountains! People look over them time and time again! They ignore their presence. Let me remind you though, a penny never loses its value. Friends, we are all valuable as children of God. Wouldn't you say that any specimen of light is considered valuable? Because God called us out of darkness into His marvelous light, we are identified with light as Christians. Therefore, when we are encompassed by any dark situation, we are a specimen of light, that particle of hope which is valuable in a darkened path. Some of you may have been beaten up by the enemy, torn down by close friends or family, or have had your own self-worth destroyed because of your past.

My brothers and sisters, no matter what your issues have been, in your wilderness experience, recognize that your value can't be taken away. God elected you! He chose you, before you chose Him. The very fact that God chose us lets me know that we are valuable. Jesus' resurrection from the dead reminds me that I was something worth dying for. Recognize and realize that you are worth more than your problems. No matter what's stuck to that penny, any cashier accepts its value over its condition. You may lose your valuables, but you won't lose your value.

Jesus posed this question in the book of Luke, "What profit is it to man if he gain the whole world and he himself is lost or destroyed?" Consider the inverse of this text: a man having nothing, but he is not destroyed. It signifies that our soul is what's important. When you feel life is hopeless, change your perception! Show others that they've mistaken your true identity. Shake off your grave clothes! Start identifying yourself as a champ when others have identified you as a chump. Start relying on the S<u>O</u>N as your source of happiness instead of the S<u>U</u>N.

DAY 16
Got Protection?

Be thankful for what you have and what you didn't end up with because there's someone worse off than you.

For the law was given through Moses, but grace and truth came through Jesus Christ.
-John 1:17

Grace is simply unmerited favor, getting things we don't deserve! It's like confessing to the jury our guilt of a crime, but we don't face the penalty of what the guidelines say. Praise God! If you could just take a moment and think about the sins that you have committed over the course of your life, within the past month, within the past week, within the past day, a few minutes ago, and even right now, and know that God still grants you grace, that should be enough to commit yourself to Him.

It's certainly enough to worship Him because there is no one else that would let us off the hook. Even God himself turns His nose up at sin, but Jesus sitting on the throne at the right hand of our father is our defense attorney. That time you slept with that person and you didn't end up with a KID or a STD. That time you drove home drunk and the police only told you your headlight was out. That time you faced maximum jail time, but got a lesser sentence or was found not guilty. That time you were late for work and upset with the world only to realize that there was an accident that occurred on your route just before your normal time of passing that intersection. Consider this, if you are not thankful for what God has done for you and has not allowed to happen to you, that's a slap in the face to God. God resists the proud and exalts the humble. Embracing humility and meekness is the way of the Christian!

DAY 17
Enough is Enough

Pain is a prerequisite for mercy. Because many become arrogant with grace, we need mercy to humble us.

Surely goodness and mercy shall follow me all the days of my life

-Psalms 23:6

As a child, two of my favorite pastimes, when there wasn't a basketball or toys, were playing mercy or thumps. We played Mercy to see who was considered the toughest because they were able tolerate pain the longest. The objective of Mercy was to bend your opponents' fingers back by locking them all together until they cried out "MERCY." My brothers and sisters, it isn't until pain is felt that the person cries out "MERCY." God's mercy is everlasting because we will forever feel the pain of some stimulus, and it's God who grants us mercy to take the pain away. We need this mercy because it sets us up for grace. God shows us mercy when we do wrong, and because we are sinners, His blessing us is a product of His goodness to us.

It is like saying, "enough is enough" because Mercy shows up when we can't handle the pain anymore. But when mercy shows up, so does grace. That's why they are twins because enough is enough, it's a double proclamation!

Enough pain yields mercy. Enough of anything good is His grace. He'll supply all of our needs according to His riches in glory. In your wilderness, know that you have backup. David says the twins will follow us! You're never alone on your wilderness. Grace and Mercy say that God will never put more on me than I can bear, even when I deserve all pain that may come my way.

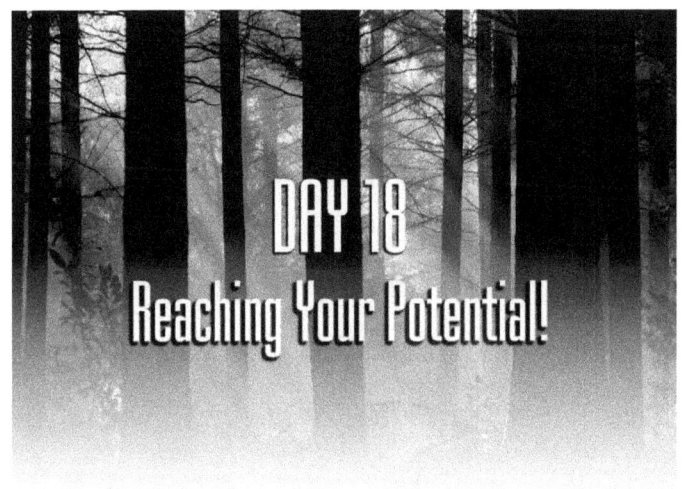

Day 18
Reaching Your Potential!

Pre-cooked food is already made! BUT, it must stand the heat to reach its potential. You may face some heated situations, but it's to reach your potential.

"Before I formed you in the womb I knew you; Before you were born I sanctified you; I ordained you a prophet to the nations."

-Jeremiah 1:5

God is saying to the prophet Jeremiah that his destiny was predetermined before he was born. God has a plan for all of our lives, and it takes us going thru some storms in order to reach our potential. I don't know where you are on your spiritual journey, but if you know God has got to have something better for you than where you are right now in your current season, stay the course and know that you are in route for destiny. Did you know that gold is shaped and formed only when it encounters heat? Once it is finished, it has a glossy finish! God has to reform us in order to see himself in us. In you spiritual wilderness be encouraged to know that God is using you for a greater good. You will be blessed and others around you will be blessed! Don't allow your neighbors, negative know-it-alls, and needless people to hinder your potential. It's so easy to quit. But there is a greater good.

Remember that heat helps form and shape metal. Remember, I told you that God says you're valuable! Remember, when you stand the heat, your value is being shaped! Beloved, God didn't bless you this much to quit on you. He didn't bring you this far to turn His back on you. He loves you! God gave us His all. Give him your all by reaching your potential.

Today is the last day for your liability insurance. You won't need it anymore because you're taking NO liabilities.

Therefore we also, since we are surrounded by so great a cloud of witnesses, let us lay aside every weight, and the sin which so easily ensnares us, and let us run with endurance the race that is set before us,

-Hebrews 12:1

On your mark, get set, go! At the sound of the gun, the runner begins running his race. The runner runs at his highest potential in order to secure victory. If indeed the runner decides that he or she wants to add extra weight to their persona, then this will indeed slow the runner down from performing at his or her maximum potential. Their concern is not about how the other runners started the race. Their only concern is reaching the finish line before their opponents. The runner realizes that the more he/she turns around and focuses on the runners behind them, or on the starting line, the more they risk losing the race.

My brothers and sisters, are you running a race trying to carry some unwanted baggage? Hebrews 12 says to let us lay aside every weight and the sin which so easily besets us! Some people and some things that we have attached ourselves to aren't good for our race of faith.

They make us struggle with challenges that may not have intended to be so complicated. We must remember that to get over something, we must displace ourselves from the element. It's difficult to get over an issue when the element of the issue is present in our lives. An alcoholic will find it extremely difficult to embrace sobriety if he spent his leisure time at the bar or liquor store. Those elements must be removed before that thing that easily besets us can be laid aside. If you're in a relationship or on a job and you feel like you haven't reached your potential, check your attachments, and don't focus on your past! Let it go!

Why did God give us two ears and one mouth? Was it because He knew we wouldn't have much to say, or was it because we need to listen more?

So then, my beloved brethren, let every man be swift to hear, slow to speak, slow to wrath; 20) for the wrath of man does not produce the righteousness of God.
-James 1:19-20

This is a question that I've wondered about for a while now, and I found it in the scriptures. When we are vocal, it is hard to listen at times. Our tongues play an important role in our speech. The tongue is a member of the body which is hard to tame. It is a very small body part, but it can cause the greatest damage. The smallest spark of fire could cause a massive blaze of flames. Our tongues work the same way. We can be forgiven, but people rarely forget what we've said. You can't take back things which are spoken. This is one of the reasons God instructs through James to be slow to speak.

Some people have talked themselves out of blessings. Have control over your words. Words can be manipulated and therefore cause drama in your life. Listen, you're already in your wilderness experience. The last thing you want to do is add fuel to the fire in your life. Saints of God can sometimes be their own worst enemy. Are you slow to anger and quick to forgive? People often fail to listen. They misunderstand things, and confusion is birthed, which may cause conflict. The bible teaches us to be slow to anger like God is. Don't let the small things stress you out and cause you to be angry.

ANGER can lead to sin, and it may cause you to miss your moment! Don't miss your moment! We are people who wear our emotions on our face. Pursue happiness; give an effort to resist anger. And if you do get angry, SIN NOT!

The rearview and side view mirrors in the car are for us to see where we came from, a flashback so to speak.

Brethren, I do not count myself to have apprehended; but one thing I do, forgetting those things which are behind and reaching forward to those things which are ahead, I press toward the goal for the prize of the upward call of God in Christ Jesus.

-Philippians 3:13-14

If you drive always looking in the rearview, you're headed for devastation. The mirrors are intended for glancing at. Don't focus on what's in the past because you may miss the opportunity God is putting right in front of you. You may have overcome some situations in your life and the enemy has revisited the situations through trickery. It is important, beloved, that you understand that your past is a past for a reason. It is simply those things that have passed. It is impossible to live in the past and prepare for the future. No one can go from past to future and not encounter the present. Your present state sets you up for the future by learning from your past. When Paul wrote to the Philippians, he knew that in order for them to proceed to newer heights, they had to reach for, not reach back. Can you imagine driving and always turning your head completely around to observe your surroundings? His timing is not ours. How many times have you been driving and missed your exit because you were busy looking at something else? Have you ever had an accident because you weren't focused on what was lying ahead? DON'T LOOK BACK because you may miss out!

Jesus' earthly job was carpentry. Ask Him to build you a bridge so that you can get over what's keeping you from your Desired Destination.

(2) And when the Sabbath had come, He began to teach in the synagogue. And many hearing Him were astonished, saying," Where did this Man get these things? And what wisdom is this which is given to Him, that such mighty works are performed by His hands! (3) Is this not the carpenter, the Son of Mary, and brother of James, Joses, Judas, and Simon? And are not His sisters here with us?" So they were offended at Him.

-Mark 6:2-3

Many Christians at one point or another in their lives claim to know what their destinies are and that God has revealed it to them. Some claim to have been called by God for certain obligations concerning the church. The question is, "What's keeping you from getting there?" Some are held up by the relationships they are in, the way they were raised, or the whole environment itself in which they reside. It's important that you reach your destiny by living out your purpose. Why let things stand in the way? Break those attachments to people who are not going anywhere that you are going. Lose those situations and environments that influence you to take your eyes off of Christ and turn your ear from His voice. As in the scripture, Jesus is able to perform mighty works with His hands.

Beloved, whatever your problem, put it all in His hands. A carpenter understands the necessity of a tool being in his or her hand in order to fix anything. Jesus, our God, has tools of wisdom to where He's omnipotent, omniscient, and omnipresent. He knows your problems, He knows how to handle them and you simultaneously, and He's just waiting on you to give Him the go-ahead to get you across your river of issues.

God works thru signs and wonders. Don't ignore the signs; it may cost you your life!

Then said Jesus unto him, Except ye see signs and wonders, ye will not believe.
                                        -John 4:48

We as living organisms have been conditioned to take notice of signs. Even animals recognize signs and commands from their trainers. A sign is simply an informational tool that informs us of a variable or directs us to an unfamiliar place. When it comes to direction, however, you may make the wrong turn that causes you to waste precious time in reaching your destination or maximizing your potential. Signs are posted and rooted because they are not intended to go anywhere and are available for a double back when we pass them by. In the event we have to double back, we pay close attention for the signs! We not only look for the sign, but we become observant and notice the environment in which the sign is positioned.

This means the building structure or landscape that it is in front of, the length it is away from your actual turn, the dynamics of the actual sign itself, and the condition of the sign. If you can't see the sign, lift up your visor and clear your windshield. Don't let anything cloud your ability to see what God is doing in your life.

And a certain woman, which had an issue of blood twelve years, And had suffered many things of many physicians, and had spent all that she had, and was nothing bettered, but rather grew worse, When she had heard of Jesus, came in the press behind, and touched his garment.

-Mark 5:25-27

Lord, forgive me for being envious of those with 4-wheel drive that just flew past me during the blizzard that winter morning. But thanks be unto

God for teaching me this lesson. Everyone was affected by the same snow. But some were able to get thru and to their destinations sooner than others by using their 4-Wheel Drive or All Wheel Drive. This woman had been sick with blood difficulties for twelve long years. She pressed her way thru the crowd to get to her destiny of reaching Jesus and being healed. It was her faith that healed her, but her condition that motivated the press. In life, our pain will activate our faith and motivate us to go into overdrive. There are times when we need to be walking completely in faith to get over obstacles. If this woman can press her way thru the crowd, then surely we can, too.

Her example serves as the tracks in the snow, indicating that when something looks noble to us, someone else has already been through the test and has served as our model to follow. When freshly fallen snow hasn't been plowed, the most successful way in traveling is to follow the tire tracks in the snow ahead of us. Lord, when we can't see our way thru or when it's tough to get to our destination, we will follow the path that you've made for us by using others who have pressed forward ahead of us.

DAY 25
Be careful!

If you confess with your mouth the Lord Jesus and believe in your heart that God has raised Him from the dead, you will be saved.

-Romans 10:-9

We are quick to tell others to be careful. Being careful is to exercise safety. Safety derives from the word safe. Safe is to be kept. To keep is to save! In your wilderness experience and even on your spiritual journey, it is important not to lose your spiritual sanity. Keep your salvation close to your heart. Your salvation should not be defined by the present situation you find yourself in. On this road, there are going to be rough days ahead. Job 14:1 says that man born of a woman is of a few days and full of trouble. Encountering difficulty is inevitable. But it is important that we keep our salvation. We spend countless years increasing our savings account. It is protocol to save all computer documents. When we don't save, we simply lose what we wanted to be stored away.

Paul is telling the Roman church that by confessing Christ as the savior and believing God sent Him and lifted Him from the grave, you will be saved from condemnation. This confessing puts you on the path for eternal life. So, take care that you don't allow life's storms to cause you to lose your salvation. If you've been backsliding from your relationship with God and the church, reactivate your relationship so that you might be saved from Hell because neither you, I, nor anyone else knows the Day of Judgment.

23) Let us hold fast the confession of our hope without wavering, for He who promised is faithful. 24) And let us consider one another in order to stir up love and good works, 25) not forsaking the assembling of ourselves together, as is the manner of some, but exhorting one another, and so much the more as you see the Day approaching.

-Hebrews 10:23-25

Many have turned to supplements and energy drinks to boost themselves and alter their state of being. But the best place for this to happen is at church. Church is designed to be the only place where you can worship God and share testimonies without offending anyone.

The body of Christ had allowed the world to dictate our conversing about Christ and with Christ in places such as schools. Church is beneficial to the believer. You are able to learn from and be encouraged by others ministering to you. You are sometimes able to (depending on the size of your church) develop and maintain a relationship with your Pastor. I like to think of church as the spiritual gas station. We run all week long, and sometimes we become overwhelmed with what life has presented us. We go to the gas station to pay for something we need to carry us from point A to point B. While the gospel of Jesus Christ is free, it is still valuable to sow monetary gifts, worship God, and help others that need to be helped in some way, shape, or form. You are sowing into the ministry for your own benefit. You will reap what you sow.

In a time where cyber church seems to be growing in popularity, remember what Hebrews 10:24-25 says, "And let us consider one another in order to stir up love and good works, not forsaking the assembling of ourselves together, as is the manner of some, but exhorting one another, and so much the more as you see the Day approaching." Go to church--your blessings are there waiting for you to claim them!

Praise the LORD! Praise God in His sanctuary; Praise Him in His mighty firmament! 2) Praise Him for His mighty acts; Praise Him according to His excellent greatness! 3) Praise Him with the sound of the trumpet; Praise Him with the lute and harp! 4) Praise Him with the timbrel and dance; Praise Him with stringed instruments and flutes! 5) Praise Him with loud cymbals; Praise Him with clashing cymbals! 6) Let everything that has breath praise the LORD. Praise the LORD!

-Psalms 150

Let everything that has breath praise the Lord. You're only excused for not praising Him when you've lost your breath. What you're going through is to intensify your praise. If you feel that you don't have anything to praise the Lord for, consider verse 2. Praise him for his mighty acts. No one else can do what God has done, is doing, and is getting ready to do, not only in your life, but in the lives of others. Who is worthy to possess excellent greatness? Michael Jordan was great, but He was excellently great! Because God is so worthy of all of our praise, whatever we have in our possession, we can praise Him with, even our problems!

So Rev., how can I praise God with my problems? God says in Psalms 150:6, "Let everything that has breath praise the Lord." Having breath is to exist. The fact that you have a problem means there's an issue that exists. Would you praise God for your breakthrough if you had nothing to break from? Lord, thank You for my problems. If I didn't have any, I'd be taking away from your character of being the problem solver. In Jesus name, Amen!

DAY 28
Leave the light on!

14) "You are the light of the world. A city that is set on a hill cannot be hidden. 15) Nor do they light a lamp and put it under a basket, but on a lampstand, and it gives light to all who are in the house. 16) Let your light so shine before men, that they may see your good works and glorify your Father in heaven.
-Matthew 5:14-16

Now is the time where your light should be shining. It can become so easy to be influenced by the enemy to shut your light off. Don't allow your circumstances to affect how you shine that little light of yours. In case you haven't realized, we are life to other people. We are life by being a light. Don't expect to see a 60-Watt light bulb glowing from my chest, but expect to hear enlightening conversation from me with those who are in a dark area of life. Please be careful to become a motion light. A motion light comes on once someone crosses its path of sensors.

Don't act Godly only in the presence of other "church folk." Letting your light shine guides those individuals who are surrounded by darkness, whether it be darkness in their family, finances, or health. People are seeking refuge from the rubble in their lives. Be a life saver by shining your light. You are the light, but every light has a power source. You remember, Jesus resurrected with all power. Show the God in you.

But thanks be to God, who gives us the victory through our Lord Jesus Christ.

- 1 Corinthians 15:57

People take for granted the small victories by failing to recognize them. They squander their time and energy trying to win the big one! Take advantage of the small victories because they are preparing you for what's too much for you to handle right now. Victory is conquest or success over *any* stimuli, whether it is winning an arm wrestling competition or a 26 mile marathon.

The fact is that there are people in this world who would love to accomplish that very thing which you considered to be minute. Children of God have been given the victory over defeat by our faithful relationship with Jesus Christ. Christ gave us the victory at Calvary's mountain in purchasing our salvation by bearing our sins, dying on the cross, and resurrecting the third morning. Although preachers and teachers teach the resurrection Sunday after Sunday, people still get caught up in defeat.

Beloved, the enemy may win some battles, but he won't win the war. You have to declare even in the midst of your spiritual wilderness that victory belongs to you. It's yours! You have it in your possession! Listen, this is your year to be victorious. It's time to change your thinking and language. Replace your vowels in words like Chump to Champ, or your Happiness for the Sun shining to the Son rising. Your victory starts in your thinking. It's time to change your perception: Instead of looking at an empty cup as having lost everything that was in it, look at is as available to refill. You've been granted the victory already; you just have to walk in it.

For all have sinned and fall short of the glory of God, (24) being justified freely by His grace through the redemption that is in Christ Jesus, (25) whom God set forth as a propitiation by His blood, through faith, to demonstrate His righteousness, because in His forbearance God had passed over the sins that were previously committed, (26) to demonstrate at the present time His righteousness, that He might be just and the justifier of the one who has faith in Jesus.

-Romans 3:23-26

Take a minute and think about what you deserve and what you don't deserve. The bible teaches us that there's no one good but one, and that's God. Neither you nor I deserve to be living. The very thoughts that we have thought, the various sins we've committed prior to picking up this book; the things that we've failed to do, they all convict us as sinners.

There are three kinds of sin: a *sin nature*, an *imputed sin*, and a *personal sin*. A sin nature is that we were shaped in iniquity like David said in Psalms 51:5. This is why the bible says in 1 John 1:10, "If we say that we have not sinned, we make Him a liar, and His word is not in us." Imputed sin is sin charged to us because of Adam. By one man's offense, sin entered the world (Romans 5:17). Let's examine personal sin. Folks like to excuse sin, but there are two types of personal sin, sin of commission and sin of omission. See, we recognize the sin of commission as doing something we shouldn't do, but a sin of omission is not doing something that is required of us to do. But praise God that He loved us so much (John 3:16) that He sent us Jesus, and Jesus stepped in and paid the cost. Talk about insurance--there's Jesus paying the price for things that we've done, and we don't even have a co-pay. Hopefully, that's enough for you to dedicate your life to being sold out for Christ.

DAY 31
A job to do!

"Then he who had received the one talent came and said, 'Lord, I knew you to be a hard man, reaping where you have not sown, and gathering where you have not scattered seed. (25) And I was afraid, and went and hid your talent in the ground. Look, there you have what is yours.'

-Matthew 25:24-25

We are now living in a society where good work is hard to find. Unemployment has skyrocketed. Although society has informed us that we are living in a recession and businesses are merging with layoffs resulting from it, there is still work to do for the child of God. Let's look at the parable of the talents. Two of the servants were profitable and one wasn't. The two that were profitable put in work to be profitable. They used what they had to get more than what they had and asked for. When you're working for the Lord, He will make you ruler over many things because of your faithful attitude over the few that you do have.

However, the one who only received one talent did nothing. He wasn't profitable, which means he didn't do what was required of him. For example, an investor gives his product to an employee. If a door-to-door salesman does not sell his product, he's not profitable and repercussions may follow. This servant had to answer to his repercussions of being unprofitable. Satan is doing his job, trying to kill, steal, and destroy the people of God! If Satan is not on your case, check your relationship with Christ because Satan won't hassle those whom he already has. The question is, are you doing your job as a Christian in the Kingdom of God, being profitable, using the gifts God has given you to minister to others His gospel? Do you know what your job is? I suggest that you read the parable of the talents. Your effort will make you ruler over things you had no idea you could rule.

So they picked up Jonah and threw him into the sea, and the sea ceased from its raging. (16) Then the men feared the LORD exceedingly, and offered a sacrifice to the LORD and took vows.

-Jonah 1:15-16

You being faced with the impossible will give God the chance to show off. It opens the door for the miraculous to occur. Jonah had made a mistake in running from God. He went the opposite direction of where God instructed him to go. Jonah found himself on a ship fleeing from his assignment. He found himself to be in a situation where his disobedience was hazardous to others around him. God had allowed a severe storm to develop while Jonah was on the ship with mariners. They were faced with an impossible situation of rowing the ship through the tempest sea. But God used Jonah even is his disobedience to show the power of the true and living God. It was at the time when the mariners threw Jonah off the ship as he requested that the tempest sea calmed. The mariners recognized God as God and gave Him the glory.

Sometimes God will use His children as vessels of Glory. It may be the will of God for storms to surface in our lives. It may be God's design that you are bothered, battered, or beaten. So many times we give up on living when dark clouds have positioned themselves in our lives. There have been countless Christians who've turned their attention away from God when times got rough. You may have to experience being broke or bruised before experiencing peace, power, and prosperity, just so others recognize that it was only God who was responsible for your breakthrough.

The Way Out is...Through

DAY 33
Divine Intervention!

Consider the snow flake. Don't you know snow flurries fall from the sky more often than not, but by the time they reach the atmosphere they melt?

20) But as for you, you meant evil against me; but God meant it for good, in order to bring it about as it is this day, to save many people alive.
-Genesis 50:20

To most bible readers, the story of Joseph is familiar to the ear. Joseph's brothers hated him because his father showed favor to him the most. Joseph also had the gift of interpreting dreams. His brothers were filled with hate and plotted to kill Joseph, but they ended up selling him to Potiphar's house. This happened in Genesis 39, but Joseph's breakthrough comes a few chapters later in which he issues this statement to his brothers in Genesis 50:20, "But as for you, you meant evil against me; but God meant it for good, in order to bring it about as it is this day, to save many people alive."

Beloved, just as with these snowflakes, what the devil had intended for you, what could have taken you out of here melted away because God changed your climate. Sometimes in life, your environment must change whether it is voluntarily or not. Your surroundings will set you up to receive the intervention of favor from God. To intervene simply means to get involved.

In order for evil to be redirected, God has to get involved, but you have to engage in the involvement. To be involved is to have a relationship. If you are waiting for God to intervene in your life, you have to consider two things. First, recognize that God's timing is not our timing. Second, recognize that involvement requires a relationship. Today, examine your relationship with God. Joseph had a relationship with God, and his behavior proved it.

DAY 34
Take Control!

When you praise, the enemy gets choked up!

8) "Judah, you are he whom your brothers shall praise; Your hand shall be on the neck of your enemies; Your father's children shall bow down before you. (9) Judah is a lion's whelp; From the prey, my son, you have gone up. He bows down, he lies down as a lion; And as a lion, who shall rouse him?

-Genesis 49:8-9

In Genesis 29:35, the bible says Leah conceived again and bore a son, and said, "Now I will praise the LORD." Therefore, she called his name Judah. Then she stopped bearing. God was praised for him, praised by him, and praised in him; and therefore his brethren shall praise him. Judah's name means praise, which is a word associated with victory.

Beloved, when "praise" is activated, your hand shall be on the neck of your enemies. When you have your hand on the neck of someone, you are in a position of control. Even in your wilderness, get your praise on. The fact of the matter is God has not changed, despite our wilderness environments. Don't lose control to the enemy by failing to praise God from whom all blessings flow. You slow down the enemy's attempt to assassinate your purpose when you praise. You block the enemy when you praise because demons tremble at the name of Jesus.

The ninth verse in the above passage says, "Judah is a lion's whelp." The lion is the king of beasts. He's the terror of the forest when he roars. When he seizes his prey, none can resist him. When he goes up from the prey, none dare pursue him for revenge. He looks strong, intimidating. By this, it is foretold that the tribe of Judah should become very formidable and should not only obtain great victories but also peaceably and quietly enjoy what was obtained by those victories. Some of us have allowed the devil to come in our lives, which has caused anomie, fracturing our families and upsetting our communities with organized crime. But your praise ought to be used to make peace.

Take control! Take back your families, your relationships, finances, and communities.

DAY 35
Activate your faith

Hey, if you could always see your way out of situations, you wouldn't please God. He puts us in situations to activate our faith so that we can please Him! Without faith, it's impossible to please God.

Now faith is the substance of things hoped for, the evidence of things not seen.
-Hebrews 11:1

It is no wonder why a person in the dark seeks the light. In fact, he unconsciously puts his faith and trust in the light, that it will not lead him to destruction but will provide the breakthrough he is seeking. Jesus explains to His listeners at the Mount of Olives in John 8:12 that He is the light of the world and that those who follow Him will not walk in darkness, but have the light of life. Jesus certainly won't lead us to destruction and leave us, and He certainly provides the breakthrough that we are seeking. We are placed in situations of darkness as a test of faith.

On your spiritual journey, realize that it is faith in which we believe what we believe (the birth, burial, and resurrection of Jesus Christ). Having a cell phone that is not activated will store numbers, but it won't serve its intended purpose, which is for communication. What's the point of confessing a faith-based religion and not activating your faith? With just an ounce of faith you can move beyond the ordinary. Don't fall into deactivation. Operate in a NOW FAITH mindset so when you fall into darkness, you're immediately activating and operating in faith, knowing that God will see you through and bring you out.

The Way Out is...Through

DAY 36
Get Up!

Now Jesus, going up to Jerusalem, took the twelve disciples aside on the road and said to them, (18) "Behold, we are going up to Jerusalem, and the Son of Man will be betrayed to the chief priests and to the scribes; and they will condemn Him to death, (19) and deliver Him to the Gentiles to mock and to scourge and to crucify. And the third day He will rise again."

-Matthew 20:17-19

The cross robbed the grave of death. Jesus told His disciples to take up their cross and follow Him. Beloved, NO CROSS, NO RESURRECTION!

Jesus' mission on earth was to eventually be crucified. He was crucified on the cross-where He purchased our salvation. Jesus forced Himself to the cross in the garden of Gethsemane. The gospel of Jesus Christ says he died on a Friday and resurrected early Sunday morning. While we love and honor Easter, Good Friday should be honored the same way because in order for Christ to be resurrected on Sunday morning, he had to die on Friday.

My brothers and sisters, I don't know what you've been through, but while you may be experiencing pain now, know that you will be resurrected. The only way for metal to take its shape is by applying the metal to a heat source such as fire, and the metal will be molded into its intended design. Stop looking at the season of your life of being betrayed and beaten as defeat.

Instead, look at your cross as your breakthrough. You're going to use your sufferings with the power of God as your basic training for your destiny. Don't let the sufferings of this present time get you off track for your resurrection. Whatever sin you have been struggling with or defines who you are, know that you'll rise above what put you under!

And we know that all things work together for good to those who love God, to those who are the called according to His purpose

-Romans 8:28

As we edge closer toward the end of the wilderness experience, let's talk about purpose. How can things that seem to be all bad work out for my good? One of the most important household items that my wife and I have purchased is an iron. It means so much to us being professionals and in ministry. But let's face it, the iron could be extremely dangerous if operated carelessly. So often we instruct others to be careful around the hot iron. But let's look at the purpose of the iron. The iron is designed to make wrinkles disappear. Some of us wouldn't dare be caught in public wearing anything that's wrinkled. The iron is successful when it's filled with water, pressed and steamed to its article.

Beloved, sometimes God will apply heat and pressure to us to iron out the wrinkles. We often times want to run away from the pressure or run away from the heat. Many use the cliché, 'if you can't take the heat, get out of the kitchen.' Let's consider staying, because like the iron, unless certain situations get intensely heated enough, the wrinkles of problems won't go anywhere. They will be forever evident. The Apostle Paul, experienced several heated situations and pressures from the community after his conversion. He even ended up in jail for doing nothing but spreading the gospel of Jesus Christ. However, it was all God's plan for Paul to take the gospel abroad. God had ironed things out with Paul. Some articles of clothing that were wrinkled before we ironed them establish a new identity once we're done ironing.

Don't waste your time focusing on finite impossibilities when you can zero in on your infinite possibilities.

I can do all things through Christ who strengthens me.
-Philippians 4:13

We live in a society that magnifies negativity. Look at your local news, for example. How often are the breaking stories something simple and positive, such as two local friends exercising conflict resolution? Not often because the negative is magnified to the point where optimism is bypassed. Beloved, don't you bypass optimism. Saying, "I can't or I won't be able to" are negative words. Who would have thought Moses would have led the children of Israel out of Egypt across the Red Sea into the wilderness away from the Egyptian army? Moses served as God's vessel of instruction, but had a speech impediment. He, too, bypassed optimism and told God he wasn't able to handle the mission. Paul declares it even with his testimony. Who would have thought, with his history, he would be a vessel for God?

    When you constantly say I can't do this or that, you are focusing on the negative, thereby wasting your time on finite impossibilities. The finite impossibilities are those fixed number of things you "can't do." Look at the unlimited amount of things you can do. The hint in the text is "through God who strengthens me."

No electronic source works independent of a supply source. There is a power source. His name is Jesus!

4) When He had stopped speaking, He said to Simon, "Launch out into the deep and let down your nets for a catch." 5) But Simon answered and said to Him, "Master, we have toiled all night and caught nothing; nevertheless at Your word I will let down the net." 6) And when they had done this, they caught a great number of fish, and their net was breaking.

-Luke 5:4-6

Sometimes in life, God throws a blessing our way that breaks us from what is routine or comfortable. So what do you do? Break normalcy and yield to what you or someone else has been praying for to happen to you? Or keep with your routine? The disciples had been toiling all night only to come up with no results. Have you ever felt like this? Have you been in a season where it just felt like things were not working out? You're putting out much effort, but not getting any results? This is how the disciples on the sea felt. They were so used to catching fish without much difficulty. In fact, it was their profession before they were called to be fishers of men. The whole point of fishing is to catch fish. Fishermen wait patiently to catch fish in a body of water (which they can't necessarily see in a boat on top of the water), and when they feel their fishing line move, they grab a hold of it.

We must be careful not to ignore the feeling that we've been waiting patiently for. After all, we might not be able to see it. It could be that job, loan, spouse, or school that we've been expecting. Beloved, God will instruct us to apply our attention to the unfamiliar or less comfortable for our own breakthrough. Some people land jobs by way of avenues they never expected. Some spouses meet their better-halves in ways that were uncomfortable for them. Don't be afraid or reluctant to follow the voice of God and move from the familiar.

DAY 40
Through it All!

28) Nebuchadnezzar spoke, saying, "Blessed be the God of Shadrach, Meshach, and Abed-Nego, who sent His Angel and delivered His servants who trusted in Him, and they have frustrated the king's word, and yielded their bodies, that they should not serve nor worship any god except their own God! 29) Therefore I make a decree that any people, nation, or language which speaks anything amiss against the God of Shadrach, Meshach, and Abed-Nego shall be cut in pieces, and their houses shall be made an ash heap; because there is no other God who can deliver like this."

-Daniel 3:28-29

Three boys in the hood find themselves in a heated situation. I can already imagine the furnace to be hot. But the King intensified the heat seven times more than normal. That was his first mistake. The number 7 represents completion. Had King Nebuchadnezzar increased the heat by any other number, perhaps there would have been different results. The fire was so hot that it killed the men who put the three Hebrew boys in the furnace.

God will protect you going into your fiery furnace because He's there waiting to be your security and comfort. David says in the 23rd number of Psalms, "Yea though I walk thru the valley of the shadows of death, I will fear no evil for thou are with me." God will send us through some valleys beyond our understanding. The plan was for the King to believe in the God of

Shadrach, Meshach, and Abed-Nego. And if the King believed, he will force the people to believe.

No one else can receive the glory of God, but sometimes in order for the glory of God to be revealed by both believers and non-believers, you may have to go through some tests, storms, and trials. Many of us ask God to use us, but fail to recognize that God sometimes uses us by taking us through the valley so that someone else sees His glory when He brings us out.

Be honored that He chose to use you, regardless of the task, because you just may be going through to reveal God's glory to others.

Conclusion

I hope and pray that after reading these words of encouragement, you've made it through your wilderness. You've made it through all the doubt, discomfort, discouragement, and dismay that you've encountered firsthand. While my struggle may have been different than yours, don't ever lose your focus! Continue to fight! Always keep the faith! You have no idea how you might encourage others in their storms.

Remember, because you may be the closer to God than others may get, always put the cross out front and showcase your strength and spirituality. For Paul said in Galatians 2:20, "I have been crucified with Christ; it is no longer I who live, but Christ lives in me."

It is my prayer that you have become stronger in faith and closer to Christ after days of reading and fasting on the word of God. I thank God for being a vessel. Hide these words in your heart and apply them when faced with the many trials, tests, and storms you'll encounter. Whatever your test, know that it has been ordained from God that you go through to get to. If people have walked out on you, given up on you, and forgotten about you, that's just your chance to be historic.

You've traveled Route 66, Psalms 66, which states in verses 10-12:

> *10 -For You, O God, have tested us; You have refined us as silver is refined.*
>
> *11 -You brought us into the net; You laid affliction on our backs.*
>
> *12 -You have caused men to ride over our heads; We went through fire and through water; But You brought us out to rich fulfillment.*

Share your experiences. Others need to hear how you made it through without breaking down. No matter the battle, know that God is bigger than your battle, and He's bringing you through to rich fulfillment. Trials come about to make you strong. Fire burns to remove impurities. God takes you through all of this just to position you into His favor, assigned and designed for your life.

Don't remove yourself! You must go through in order to get to your destiny. Keep the faith, and may the peace of the Lord God be with you now and forever.

If you want to accept Jesus Christ as your Lord, your Savior, sincerely pray this prayer and find a church home:

Prayer

Lord, forgive me for the sins that I've committed, known and unknown to me.
I confess you now as my God.
I believe that Jesus paid the price to purchase my salvation.
I believe His resurrection on the third day morning delivered me from the hands of the enemy. Lord, forgive me as I forgive others who've trespassed against me.
Show me how to be more like You.
Thank You for always loving me just the way I am.
From this point on, help me to be better.
Help me to learn from my mistakes.
Lord, I want to be a Christian.
It's in Jesus' name that I pray, Amen.

SPECIAL ACKNOWLEDGEMENTS

First and foremost, I'd like to thank God for using me. He's allowed me to experience so much in my life that I can't help but acknowledge Him through the sunshine and rain for the good times, heartaches, and pain. To my beautiful wife, Kimberly, thank you for loving me and sharing me with ministry. You helped me put it all together! To my children DaRon and Kymiah, you are the joy in my life. I love you! To my parents, Pastor Arthur C. Willis, Sr., and First Lady Janice Willis, thank you for establishing me in the way that you've reared me. You've put the fear of God in me from the time I was 3 years old, and I thank you for that. Thank you for the spiritual guidance and support that you offered me in the difficult times of my life. To my big sister, Stephanie, thank you for being a second mother to me. To Artie, thanks man, for everything. In your words, sometimes it takes God removing people in our lives in order to use us the way He wants.

Chauncey, thanks for all the support and the listening ear throughout all my ups and downs! Thanks to E.L. (Pastor Ezra Tillman), Terry (Rev. Terrance Johnson), and Kenny (Rev. Kenneth Pierce, II) for all the prayers and the brotherhood that we've formed in both life and ministry. And a special thanks to the Pentecost Missionary Baptist Church family, HYPE for Christ Youth Ministry, and Pastor JH Johnson. I must thank Pastor Jerome Farris and Pastor Jake Gaines, Jr., for inspiring me as a writer and guiding me in the process of getting my first book published. To the Pastors and ministers of the Concerned Council of Baptist Pastors and Ministers of Detroit and Vicinity, thank you all. To Ray Glandon for editing the work of this book, thank you. To Steven Lawrence Hill, Sr., and ASA Publishing, thank you for your great work and support! And lastly, to all family and friends, you have all been an inspiration to me!

www.ingramcontent.com/pod-product-compliance
Lightning Source LLC
Chambersburg PA
CBHW070641050426
42451CB00008B/247